J   Miotto, E. (Enrico)
523   The universe : origins and evolution / by Enrico
.1   Miotto ; English translation by Rocco Serini. -- Austin,
Mio   Tex. : Raintree Steck-Vaughn, c1995.
              45 p. : ill. -- (Beginnings)

          Includes bibliographical references (p. 43) and index.
          07690576   LC:94003839   ISBN:081143334X (lib. bdg.)

          1. Cosmology. 2. Astronomy. I. Title

AJAX
PUBLIC LIBRARY

447   95JAN31   43/mb   1-01040233

THE UNIVERSE

ORIGINS AND EVOLUTION

EVOLUTION OF THE UNIVERSE

4.5 billion years ago the oceans and first landmasses form. ◄ 9

1 million years after the Big Bang, hydrogen atoms form. ◄ 5

10-20 billion years ago, in less than a second, four things happen.

1. The Big Bang
2. Inflation
3. The beginning of the four forces
4. The first atomic nuclei form

1 billion years after the Big Bang, galaxies begin to form. ◄ 6

8 — 4.6 billion years ago the Earth's crust forms.

7 — 5 billion years ago the planet Earth forms.

11 — 2.5 billion years ago the atmosphere forms.

10 — 3 billion years ago bacteria appear— life begins.

BEGINNINGS

THE UNIVERSE
ORIGINS AND EVOLUTION

by
Enrico Miotto

English Translation by Rocco Serini

RSVP
**RAINTREE
STECK-VAUGHN**
P U B L I S H E R S
The Steck-Vaughn Company

Austin, Texas

Published by Raintree Steck-Vaughn Publishers, an imprint of Steck-Vaughn Company

Series Editor: Caterina Longanesi
American Edition, Edit and Rewrite: Susan Wilson
Consultant: Colton Tullen, Former Chairman, Department of Physics/Engineering Science, County College of Morris
Project Manager: Julie Klaus
Electronic Production: Scott Melcer
Cover Artwork: Maurizio Gradin and Fabio Jacomelli

Graphics and Layout: The Graphics Department of Jaca Book
Special thanks to the Museum of Natural History of Milan

Photographs: Associated Press: p. 21 (2). Italian Astrophiles: p. 9 (4), p. 32 (1). ALBERTO CONTRI, Milan: p. 21 (4). GIUSEPPI GAVAZZI, Astronomical Observatory of Brera, Milan: p. 28 (2). Hale Observatories: p. 30 (5), p. 31 (2). HALTON ARP: p. 29 (7). Editoriale Jaca Book, Milan (Carlo Scotti): p. 39 (5). Kitt Peak National Observatory: p. 14 (1), p. 28 (1), p. 29 (4). Lick Observatory: p. 31 (6). PETER MENZEL/GRAZIA NERI, Milan: p. 13 (4). EMILIO MOLINARI, Astronomical Observatory of Brera, Milan: p .29 (5). Mt. Palomar Observatory; p. 28 (3), p. 33 (2, 4). NASA: p. 13 (6, 7), p. 23 (3), p. 30 (1), p. 31 (4), p. 35, p. 39 (4). NASA/JPL: p. 38 (1, 2). National Radio Astronomy Observatory; p. 29 (8). Paris Observatory (J. M. Malherbe): p. 30 (3). Astrophysical Observatory of Arcetri, Florence: p. 8 (2), p. 23 (2). RAYMOND J. TALBOT JR., REGINALD J. DUFOUR, ERIC B. JENSEN, Rice University: p. 29 (6). United States Naval Research Laboratory; p. 9 (3).
Illustration p.13 from The New Technology Telescope ESO, January 1990.
Illustration p. 24 (1) Le Scienze, October 1992, p. 28.

Illustrations: Harvard-Smithsonian Astrophysical Observatory: p. 34-35 (1). National Institute of Anthropology and History, Mexico City: p. 10-11 (3). Editoriale Jaca Book, Milan (Giovanna Belcastro): p. 21 (3); (Sandro Corsi): p. 8-9 (1), p. 10 (2), p. 11 (4), p. 12 (3), p. 23 (4); (Cesare Dattena): p. 14-15 (2), p. 39 (3), p. 46-47; (Maurizio Gradin and Fabio Jacomelli): p. 14 (3), p. 15 (4, 5), p. 16-17, p. 18-19, p. 22 (1), p. 25 (3), p. 26-27, p. 32-33 (3), p. 36-37, p. 40-41; (Rosalba Moriggia and Maria Piatto): p. ii-iii, p. 20-21.
Illustration p. 10-11 (1) Jean-Louis de Cenival, Egypte, Époque Pharaonique, Office du Livre, Fribourg 1964, p. 86
Illustration p. 12 (2) Hevelius, Machinae Coelestis, 1673.
Illustration p. 24 (2) *New Scientist*, August 10, 1991, p. 35.

Library of Congress Cataloging-in-Publication Data

Miotto, E. (Enrico)
      [Universo. English]
      The universe: origins and evolution / by Enrico Miotto.
            p.   cm. — (Beginnings)
      Translation of: L'Universo.
      Includes index.
      ISBN 0-8114-3334-X
      1. Cosmology — Juvenile literature.   2. Astronomy — Juvenile literature.
[1. Cosmology.   2. Universe.   3. Astronomy.]   I. Title.
QB983.M5613   1995
523.1—dc20   94-3839
                                                                          CIP
                                                                          AC

Printed and bound in the United States

1 2 3 4 5 6 7 8 9 0 KP 99 98 97 96 95 94

TABLE OF CONTENTS

THE UNIVERSE

What do you see when you look up at the night sky? You mainly see stars and galaxies, the large group of stars, gases, and dust. But if you look carefully with powerful telescopes, you may be able to see clouds of dust and gas. All these things are part of the universe.

In fact, the universe includes everything—planets, stars, galaxies, dust, and gas. But it also includes the light and other forms of energy given off by stars, as well as the space through which light travels.

Light is the form of electromagnetic radiation that allows us to see. What we see is the light given off by an object or the light reflected from it. Light travels from the object to our eyes, where we form an image of the object.

Although we are not usually aware of it, we see things as they were—not as they are. The reason for this is that it takes time for light to travel. If an object is nearby, such as across a room or across a field, we can see an action almost as soon as it takes place. The reason for this is that light travels so fast—186,000 miles per second. However, the light we see outdoors during the day left the sun eight minutes before. If someone pulled down an imaginary shade to cover the sun, eight minutes would pass before it suddenly became dark! If an object is very far away, such as a distant **galaxy**, we see it as it was millions of years ago. By looking at distant heavenly bodies, we are actually looking back in time, toward the beginning of the universe, billions of years in the past.

2

1. Because the universe is so large, distances in space are not measured in miles or kilometers. Instead, distance is measured in light-years, the distance light can travel in one year. The nearest star outside our solar system is four light-years away. Galaxies outside our own Milky Way can be millions to hundreds of millions of light-years away. And quasars, the most distant heavenly bodies, are billions of light-years away.

2. For centuries, people have studied the stars in the night sky. Many of the stars seem to form patterns, which are called constellations. The stars forming a constellation only appear to be relatively close together—actually they may be widely separated in our galaxy, called the Milky Way. This is the constellation Taurus.

3. The dumbbell-shaped pattern is a cloud of gas and dust. Surrounding this cloud is the constellation of Vulpecula, which is called the Little Fox.

4. The Andromeda galaxy, a little more than two million light-years away. On clear nights during fall and winter, this galaxy can be seen without the aid of a telescope. It looks like a bright cloud in the sky.

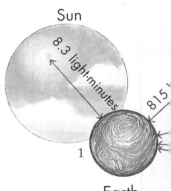

Sun

8.3 light-minutes

81.5

1

Earth

Rigel

Galaxy M81

ion light-years

Quasar 4 CO5.34

10 billion light-years

roxima Centauri
4.3 light-years

3

4

Old Ideas about the Universe

For thousands of years people have looked up in the sky and wondered about what they saw. What are the twinkling objects in the sky? Do the sun and moon move around the Earth? And for thousands of years they proposed answers to their questions.

In the distant past, people had no **telescopes** or other special equipment to help them study the sky. All they knew was based on what they could see with the "naked eye" and what they could imagine. In general, they thought that stars were the most distant heavenly bodies. But they thought the stars were much closer to Earth than they actually are. Often they thought that the sky was a dome, or bowl-shaped roof, above the Earth and that the stars hung from this dome.

The sun and moon were thought to be the most important bodies in space because they were the largest. They were thought to revolve around the Earth, which they believed was the center of the universe. Ancient people also studied the planets and saw that their positions in the sky changed compared to that of the stars.

Although many different groups of ancient peoples had different ideas about the universe, there was one common theme. Almost all believed that the universe was created by a god or gods, and for this reason they believed that the universe had a beginning.

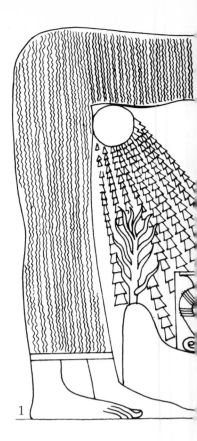

1. Like many ancient peoples, the Egyptians believed that the universe was made up of a series of layers—the sky, the Earth, and an underground world. In their myths, the sun god, Amon-Re, sprang from the stomach of the goddess of the sky, Nut.

4. The universe according to the model of the ancient Greek philosopher Aristotle. The Earth is in the center of the universe and around it revolve eight crystalline spheres that carry the moon, the sun, Mercury, Mars, Jupiter, and Saturn, while the outermost sphere, the outer circle, carries the stars. This model, with later contributions from Ptolemy in the second century A.D., was the only theory of the universe accepted in Europe for almost two thousand years.

5. Copernicus' model of the solar system taken from an atlas of 1708. The sun is in the center with the Earth revolving around it. This model, which was introduced by Copernicus in 1543, was not accepted until the 17th century.

2. Stone carvings and cave paintings often show images of heavenly bodies. This stone shows a symbol in the upper left that can stand for the sun, heat, light, or the sky. Although they may be difficult to translate, many ancient drawings give precise information on astronomical events.

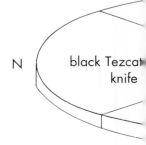

N   black Tezcat
knife

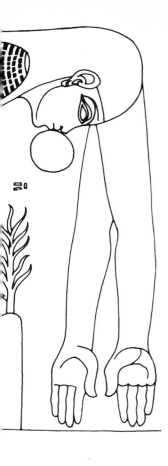

3. The Aztecs of the 12th to 15th centuries believed in a layered universe made up of thirteen heavens, one Earth layer, and nine underground worlds. In the center of the Earth layer was the main temple, shown here. Each of the four directions surrounding the temple was represented by a different color, symbol, and god.

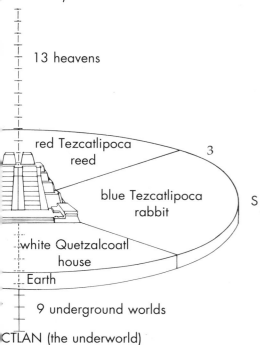

MEYOCAN
e heavens)

13 heavens

red Tezcatlipoca
reed

blue Tezcatlipoca
rabbit

3

S

white Quetzalcoatl
house

Earth

9 underground worlds

CTLAN (the underworld)

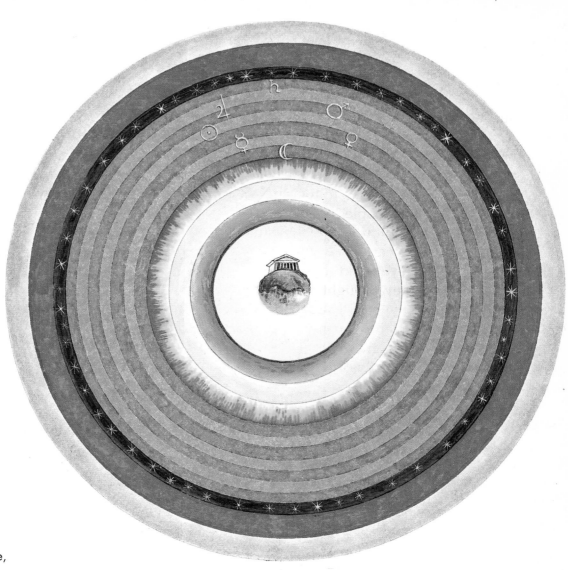

4

5

11

TELESCOPES

Although people have been studying heavenly bodies for thousands of years, they have had the use of telescopes for only the last few hundred. A great Italian scientist named Galileo Galilei made and used the first telescope in 1609. This telescope was a simple system of lenses that magnified objects by only a power of three. But it was only the beginning of a string of devices that would aid scientists in their study of space.

Later telescopes focused light with a system of mirrors. The larger the mirror, the more scientists could see with it. One of the largest mirrors was built for the Hale telescope at Palomar Observatory in California. This 200-inch diameter mirror was constructed so carefully that it took workers 11 years to cool the glass casting and to grind and polish its surface to the exact, specified shape. These huge mirrors not only increased the size of the image, but also increased its brightness.

In addition to perfecting the telescopes themselves, scientists found another way to enhance, or improve, images of the stars. Shortly after photography was invented, astronomers used it to record what they saw in the sky. By using very sensitive film and exposing it for long periods of time, they could study images that had earlier been too far away, and therefore too faint to see.

Along with light, other forms of radiation, including radio waves and X rays, are given off by stars. Special equipment can be used to record this radiation and get additional information about the universe.

ARMILLÆ ÆQVATORIÆ

1

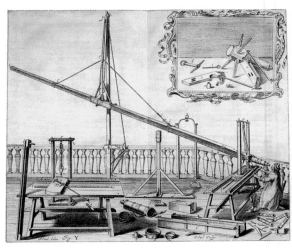

2

1. Armillary sphere, which gives the position of heavenly bodies, from the 16th century.
2. Telescope from the 17th century.
3. Beijing Astronomical Observatory from the 18th century.
4. Modern radio telescopes in New Mexico.
5. Plan for a new type of telescope to be set up in Chile.
6. Clearer images can be received from telescopes located outside Earth's atmosphere, such as this orbiting telescope which picks up infrared rays.
7. The space laboratory Skylab, which disintegrated in 1979 when it unexpectedly reentered the Earth's atmosphere.

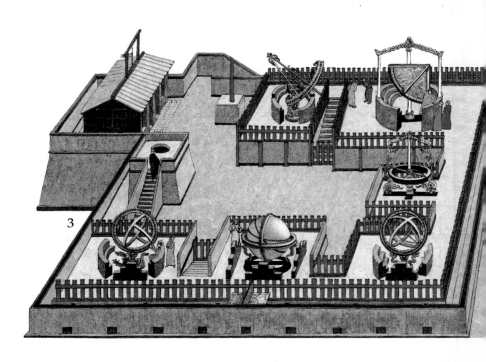

3

5

6

7

13

AN EXPANDING UNIVERSE

What can a scientist learn from looking at the night sky? The American astronomer Edwin Hubble learned about the nature of the universe by studying the colors of galaxies. Although the light from a star or galaxy may appear white, white light is made up of many different colors, like the colors of the rainbow. And the colors of distant galaxies have changed by the time we see them on Earth. Sometimes galaxies appear redder, others appear bluer.

Hubble found that more galaxies had shifted to red than to blue, and that the galaxies farthest away were the reddest. These facts are important because a light moving toward you seems to turn blue, while a light moving away from you gets redder. In other words, most of the galaxies in the universe appear to be moving away from the Earth, and those that are the farthest away are moving the fastest.

What would explain this movement? Hubble proposed that the entire universe was expanding. If that were the case, no matter where you were, everything else would appear to be moving away from you.

To understand this idea, you can compare the universe to a loaf of raisin bread. As the bread bakes, it rises, or expands. Imagine that each raisin is a galaxy. When the dough is flat, all the raisins are relatively close together. But as the dough rises, all the raisins move out and away from each other.

2. In the illustration, our own galaxy, the Milky Way, is shown in the large square and four other examples of galaxies are shown in the smaller squares. The colored lines are spectra, the patterns of light coming from each galaxy. The position of the dark bands on the spectra show a type of atom or chemical element present in each galaxy. But since the galaxies are moving away from us, the positions of the bands on the spectra have changed. Those galaxies that are the farthest away are moving away the fastest. The "redshift" of these galaxies is the greatest because they are moving the fastest. The red arrows show the distance from the Earth to each galaxy, and the the black lines show the speed at which they are moving away. Notice that as the distance increases, the speed increases.

3. The universe expands like a loaf of raisin bread rising in the oven.

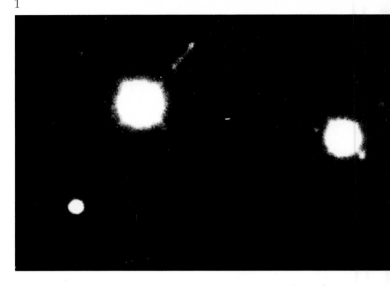

1. Photograph of Quasar number 3C273, one of the first to be identified. The word *quasar* comes from the initials QSO, for quasi-stellar object. Quasars are thought to be the extremely bright nuclei of very distant galaxies, as far as millions of light-years away. In the photograph of 3C273, a jet of gas is escaping from an object in the sky.

4., 5. Because the universe is expanding, all the galaxies move away from each other. Although we see other galaxies moving away, this does not mean that the Milky Way is the center of the universe. If we were in another galaxy, the Milky Way would appear to move away exactly as the other galaxies do.

2

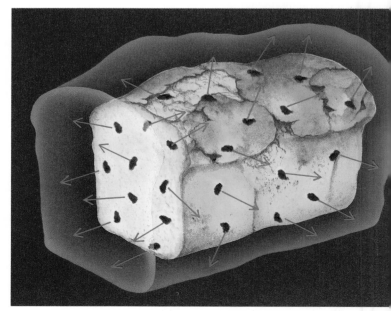

3

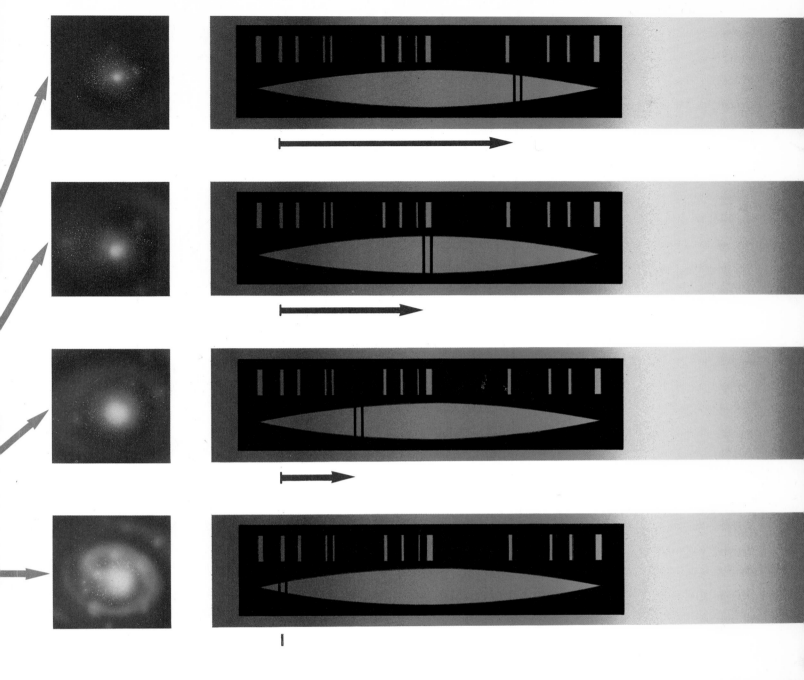

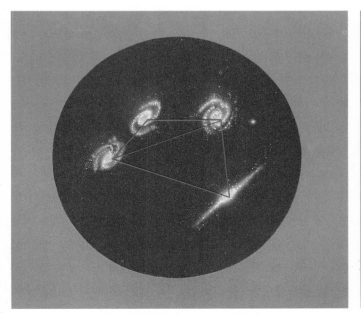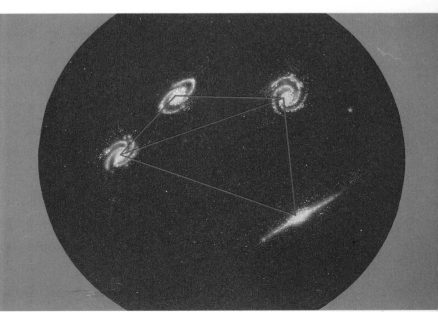

FROM THE BIG BANG...

Since ancient times, people have wondered where they came from and how their world came to be. Did the universe always exist? Was it created, or did it just happen?

For each of these questions, people have suggested answers. Now scientists believe that the universe did begin—with a bang! The Big Bang theory suggests that there was an incredibly massive explosion about 15 to 20 billion years ago. From the explosion of a super-dense fireball, all matter and space was created. The Big Bang led to the formation of the universe. This includes galaxies and all the stars, planets, moons, and clouds of dust and gas that make them up. The universe also includes large seemingly empty spaces that may be filled with matter yet to be identified.

Within an infinitesimally small fraction of a second after the Big Bang, several things happened. In the first 10^{-30} second, there was a very short period of violent expansion, called the inflation. Then within the first 10^{-10} second, the basic **forces** of nature appeared. These forces are gravitational force, the strong nuclear force, the weak nuclear force, and the electromagnetic force. Within 3 minutes after the Big Bang, the basic parts of **atoms**—the protons, neutrons, and electrons—formed.

Following this rapid succession of events there was a time span of about 300,000 years before atoms of the two simplest elements, hydrogen and helium, formed. About 1 billion years after the Big Bang, clouds of hydrogen and helium began to compact and form galaxies. As a result of the overall expansion, all the galaxies moved away from each other. This is continuing today.

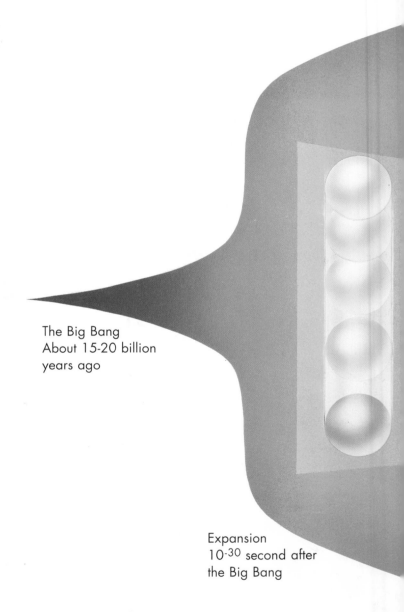

The Big Bang
About 15-20 billion years ago

Expansion
10^{-30} second after the Big Bang

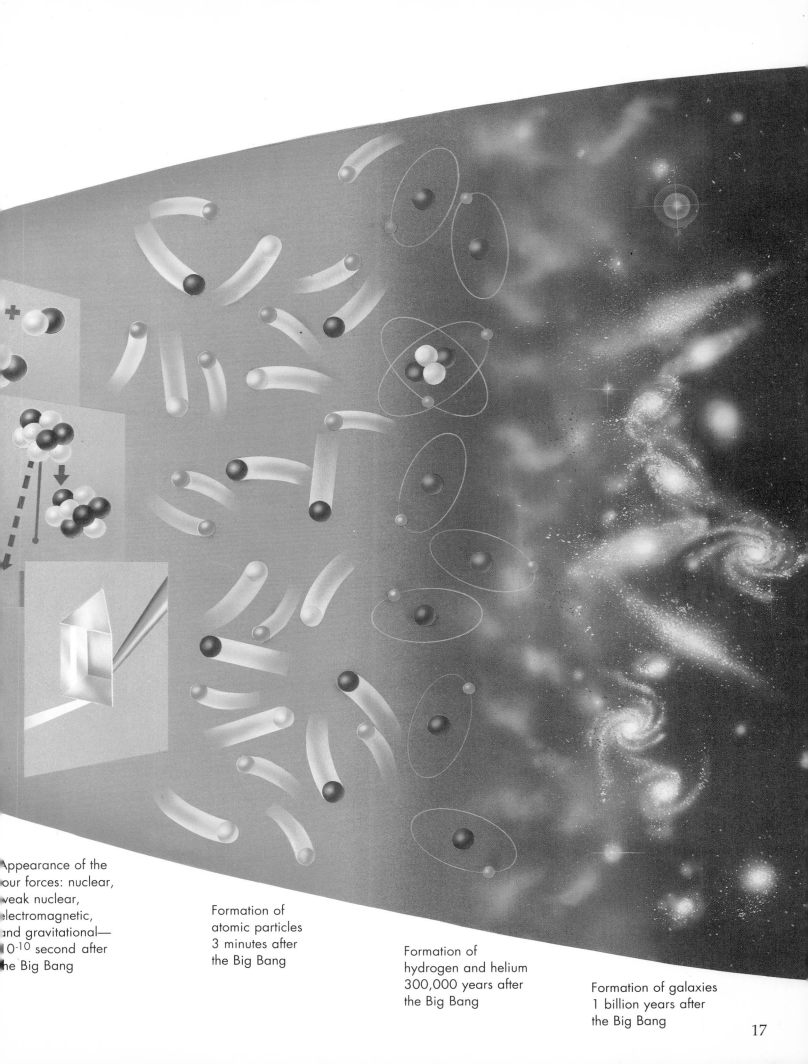

Appearance of the
four forces: nuclear,
weak nuclear,
electromagnetic,
and gravitational—
10^{-10} second after
the Big Bang

Formation of
atomic particles
3 minutes after
the Big Bang

Formation of
hydrogen and helium
300,000 years after
the Big Bang

Formation of galaxies
1 billion years after
the Big Bang

Expansion of the universe

...TO THE UNIVERSE TODAY

Today the universe appears to be a very complex structure. The galaxies are not evenly spaced, or even randomly spaced, throughout the great expanse of the universe. Instead, you could compare the structure of the universe to that of a sponge, with large empty areas. Galaxies are arranged along long, imaginary strings. In some places huge numbers of galaxies form walls that surround vast, seemingly empty spaces. What these spaces may hold is still puzzling scientists.

Sponge-like structure of the universe today

19

BEYOND THE BANG

Edwin Hubble and other scientists have found evidence that the universe is expanding. From this evidence we can reason that the universe must have been much smaller in the past. In fact, it may have been compacted into a single, super-dense fireball which then exploded with a bang and expanded into the universe as we know it. Scientists cannot really describe the Big Bang, nor what might have been before it. But scientists have a great deal of insight into what happened since then.

Within a fraction of a second after the Big Bang, the universe violently expanded. At this time there was only one force. Then as the universe expanded, it began to cool down. And in less than one one-billionth of a second, the four fundamental forces in the universe—gravity, strong nuclear, weak nuclear, and electromagnetic forces—began to operate.

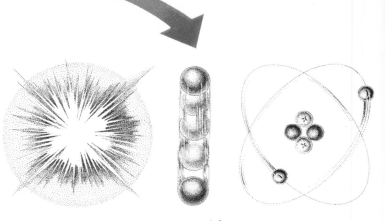

The Big Bang   Gravitational force   Atoms

1. Gravity is the attracting force between any two objects, with the more massive object having more gravitational force. Gravity pulls a ball to the ground. It also holds the planets in orbit and pulls meteorites through the atmosphere.
2. Strong nuclear force holds protons and neutrons together within the nucleus of an atom. Although this is the strongest force, it has the shortest range. It is seen when protons and neutrons bind in fusion and when they break apart in fission. The sun's energy is produced by fusion; the energy from fission can be used to create an atomic explosion.
3. Weak nuclear force can change neutrons to protons. As these changes take place within the nucleus, the chemistry of the element changes. One type of change, radioactive decay, is observed by scientists to find the age of fossils. A constant percentage of the radioactive element carbon 14, or C^{14}, is found in all living things. But when a tree dies, for example, it no longer takes in C^{14}. Since C^{14} is radioactive, the amount found in the tree begins to decrease. The half-life of C^{14} is 5,730 years, so that half of the original amount of C^{14} has changed to a new element in 5,730 years. If the tree is about 11,400 years old, then only one-quarter of its original C^{14} remains.
4. Electromagnetic force attracts objects having opposite charges and repels those having the same charge. Also, this force attracts a paper clip to a magnet. Sunlight is dispensed into its component colors: red, orange, yellow, green, blue, violet. In nature, this same process produces a rainbow.

1

Background radiation

Galaxies

The universe today

neutron
N14
C14
H
O
O

5,730 years
1/2 C14

17,190 years
1/8 C14

Over 50,000
years: almost
no C14

1

2

3

4

2

3

4

FROM PROTONS TO IRON

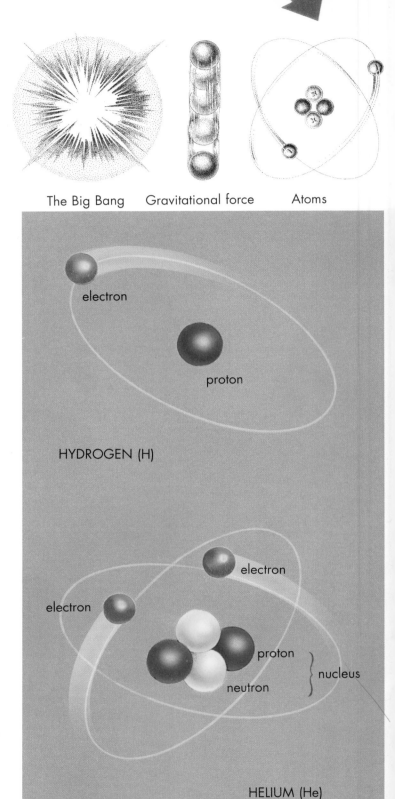

The Big Bang   Gravitational force   Atoms

Scientists believe that the temperature during the Big Bang was at least 100 billion degrees. At that temperature, matter as we know it cannot exist—there was only energy. But as cooling began during the expansion, extremely small particles of matter began to form. In less than one-hundredth of a second after the Big Bang, protons, neutrons, and electrons formed.

An atom, the incredibly small building block that makes up all things on Earth, is made up of a nucleus that is surrounded by an electron cloud. The electron cloud is made up of tiny negatively charged particles that swarm around the nucleus. Within the nucleus there are one or more protons and usually about the same number of neutrons. The proton is positively charged and the neutron, as its name suggests, is neutral.

Because all protons have the same positive charge, the electromagnetic force causes them to repel each other. But temperatures over 1 billion degrees cause them to collide violently. Then the strong nuclear force takes over and fuses them together. In this way the nucleus of an atom can form. Fusion of protons is the basic starting point of all elements, from helium to carbon to iron.

At first, there were only hydrogen and helium nuclei. Then, within 300,000 years, temperatures cooled enough to permit electrons to enter orbits around these nuclei, forming the first atoms.

HYDROGEN (H)

electron

proton

electron

electron

proton

neutron

nucleus

HELIUM (He)

1. The simplest atom is hydrogen, with a single proton in its nucleus, no neutron, and one electron in its cloud. Helium is the next simplest, with two protons, two neutrons, and two electrons.

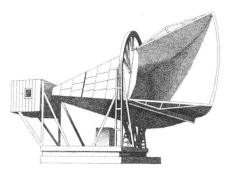

Background radiation

Galaxies

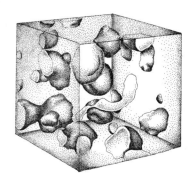

The universe today

2

4

3

2. The night sky in the constellation Cygnus, the Swan. All elements are formed in stars by nuclear reactions. In fusion, protons and neutrons join to form the nuclei of larger atoms. Elements as heavy as iron form with stars. The heavier elements form when certain stars have reached the end of their lives and explode.

3. Many of the nuclear reactions within stars give off energy. Some of this energy is given off as visible light and other forms of electromagnetic waves. Energy given off by the sun supports life on Earth. To the left is a photograph of the sun made in the ultraviolet portion of the spectrum.

4. Shown here is a sample of a few of the 103 known elements. Plutonium is an artificially created radioactive element used in nuclear weapons and nuclear-powered electrical generating stations.

WHISPERINGS FROM THE BEGINNING OF TIME

Immediately after the Big Bang, in the first fraction of time, the universe was filled with light coming from every direction. There was a fog of energy radiating from all parts. Then when the universe began to cool, some of the energy converted into matter, and the first steps toward the formation of atoms began. These first atoms—hydrogen and helium—formed large clouds that moved out and away as the universe began to expand. Also as a result of expansion, the radiating energy moved away. In time the radiation became weaker and weaker and spread farther and farther away and cooled.

Today this earliest radiation can be observed by sensitive radio receivers as background radiation. In fact, that is the way it was discovered in 1965. Two scientists at Bell Laboratories in New Jersey were troubled by "noise" in a sensitive new antenna they had built. No matter how they tried to change their instrument, there was always a faint static that seemed to come from all parts of the sky.

Other scientists had earlier predicted this background radiation as one more piece of evidence of the Big Bang. While they were searching for these waves, the scientists at Bell Labs made their accidental discovery.

Radio waves coming from all directions support the theory that the universe is expanding. Radiation from the Big Bang would extend out to the farthest reaches of the universe. Just as we can view light that originated billions of years ago, so too can we hear the earliest signals. Through advances in instrumentation technology, it has become possible to hear even incredibly weak background radio noise surviving from the Big Bang so very long ago.

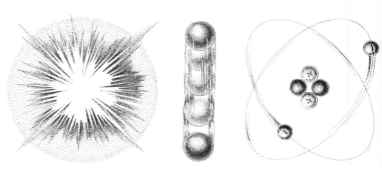

The Big Bang   Gravitational force   Atoms

1

2

1. Arno Penzias and Robert Wilson of Bell Laboratories designed the radio antenna that sensed the faint signals of background radiation.

Background radiation

Galaxies

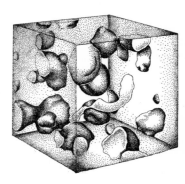

The universe today

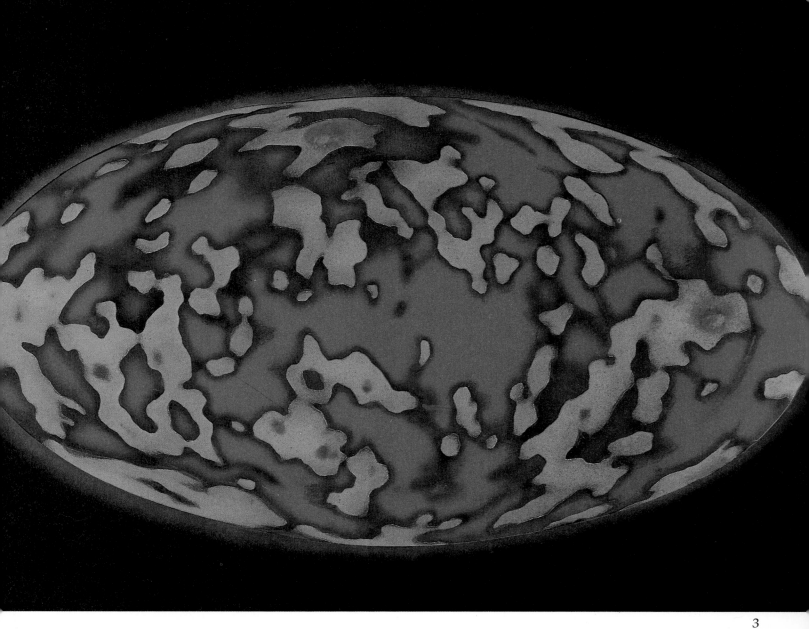

2. The satellite COBE (Cosmic Background Explorer), launched in 1989, measured background radiation that has traveled from all parts of space. Having completed its mission, it was shut down in December 1993.

3. A map of background radiation generated by data from COBE. Differences in the intensity of the radiation may show clouds of matter.

3

THE FORMATION OF GALAXIES

The Big Bang   Gravitational force   Atoms

Not long after the Big Bang, large clouds made up mainly of hydrogen gas began to form. Gravity began to have an effect, pulling the **mass** together and causing it to spin. As it spun, the cloud flattened into a huge spiraling disk, beginning the formation of a galaxy.

Within the huge spinning cloud, smaller whirlpools formed. As a whirlpool spun, gravity caused it to compact. And as its gravity increased, it spun faster and faster, pulling more and more hydrogen into the center of the whirlpool. Here at the center, hydrogen nuclei were brought into close contact, where they fused together and gave off energy. This was the beginning of the first stars in the first galaxies.

One of the many stars that formed in this way is our sun, which seems so massive to us, but is only a medium-sized star in the **Milky Way** Galaxy. Although our solar system is only about 5 billion years old, our galaxy is very old. The oldest stars of the Milky Way form a "halo" around the structure. Within this halo are clusters of stars that make up spiral-shaped arms that extend from the main mass of the galaxy. Like many other galaxies, the center of the Milky Way is densely packed with stars and is very bright.

1

2. A side view of the Milky Way, showing its flattened shape.

1. The evolution of the Milky Way. A large cloud of gas swirls through space. As it rotates, its center becomes dense, and the entire cloud flattens into a massive disk. Where the gas is most dense, stars begin to form. Clusters of stars appear in spiraling arms around the core of the galaxy.

26

2

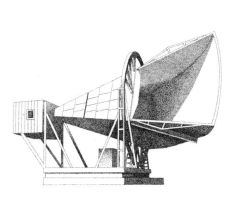

Background radiation

Galaxies

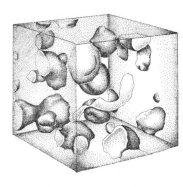

The universe today

Sun

Nebula

Clusters of
young stars

Concentrations
of stars

Area in which
stars are hidden

Interstellar gas

Detail of the
Milky Way

3. A view of some of the celestial objects within the arms of the Milky Way. The black cones to the right and left of the sun show areas where dark clouds of gas hide stars and other objects from view.

3

TYPES OF GALAXIES

The Milky Way is only one of many spiral-shaped galaxies in the universe. Typically these galaxies have several arms that stretch out over wide areas. These spiral galaxies also share the traits of being flattened disks with dense masses of stars and gas at their centers.

Another type of galaxy with spiraling arms is the barred spiral galaxy. Unlike the other galaxies, the barred spiral galaxy has only two arms, which extend from the ends of a broad and dense band of stars.

A type of galaxy with no spiraling arms is the elliptical galaxy. As a rule, this large collection of stars is smaller than a spiral galaxy.

Some galaxies do not fit into any of these categories. Galaxies like the two "Clouds of Magellan" that orbit around the Milky Way are very small. Other galaxies have irregular shapes and may be very large. Still other galaxies are unusual in the type of energy they release. While most galaxies give off light as well as other forms of **electromagnetic radiation**, one type gives off most of its energy in the form of radio waves only.

1. Typical spiral-shaped galaxy.
2. Computer-produced picture of a spiral-shaped galaxy.
3. Barred galaxy in the Coma of Berenices.
4. Elliptical galaxy.
5. Computer-produced picture of an elliptical galaxy.
6. The galaxy Centaurus A, which has features of both elliptical and spiral galaxies.
7. Computer-produced picture of an unusual spiral galaxy in which the arms extend from the center in straight lines.
8. The radio galaxy Cygnus A. Radio waves cannot be seen but can be detected with a radio telescope. This radio map was made by using a radio telescope.

Spiral
1

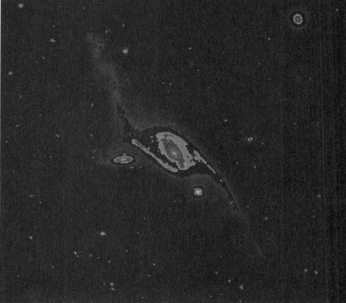

2

Barred spiral
3

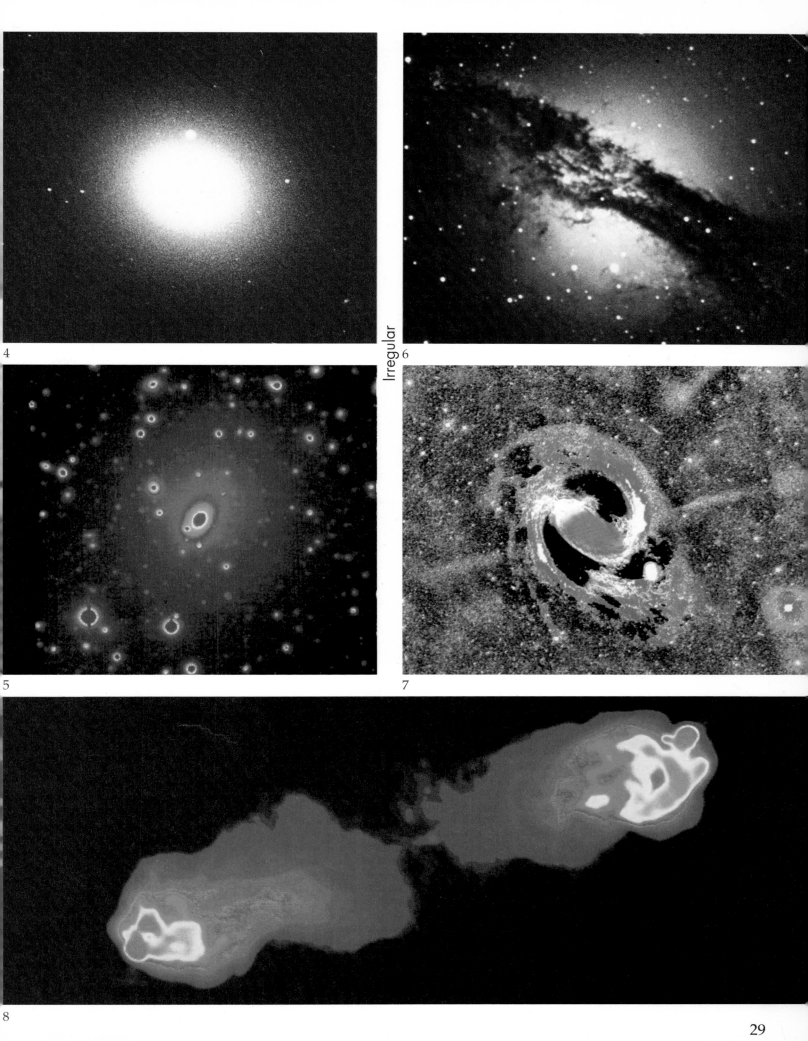

4

5

Irregular

6

7

8

29

The Life of a Star

Within a **nebula**, or cloud of gas and dust from which a **constellation** is born, many stars may form. Parts of the nebula become dense, causing gravity to pull still more matter into these regions. As gravity causes the regions to shrink, the temperature rises, causing hydrogen (protons) to fuse together, forming helium.

Once these **nuclear reactions** begin, a star is born. The reactions give off a tremendous amount of energy, which counteracts the force of gravity and keeps the star from shrinking. Some of the energy is released in the form of visible light, which gives Earth daylight from the sun and makes stars shine in the night sky.

Millions to billions of years later, the nuclear reactions slow down and give off less energy. At this point the force of the energy pushing out from the star's center is less than its gravitational force. This causes the star to shrink and compact. Another result is that there are more nuclear reactions, and the star expands into what is known as a **red giant**.

In time, the fuel of a red giant will also be used up. What happens next depends on the size of the star. A small star will collapse into a still smaller, very hot star called a **white dwarf**. A large star will collapse and then explode into a **supernova**, which can be viewed on Earth as it suddenly gives off thousands of times more light. Some supernovas then collapse into **pulsars**. Pulsars are the very small bodies which spin very rapidly and give off bursts of radio signals. The largest stars form supernovas and then shrink down again into a super-dense mass from which nothing, not even light, can escape. Since these give off no light or other electromagnetic waves, these former stars are invisible and are called **black holes**.

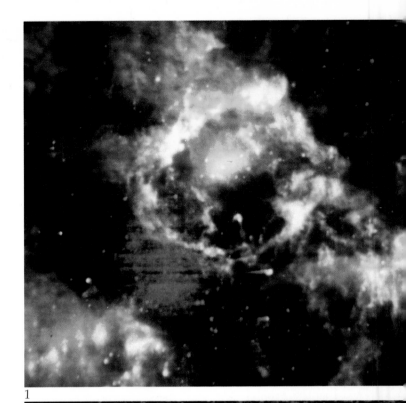
1

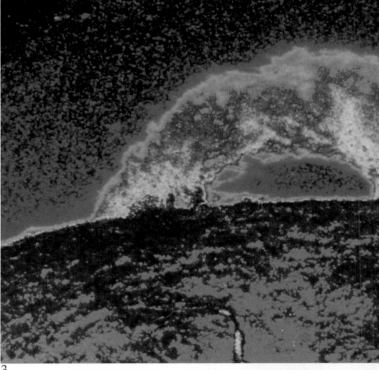
3

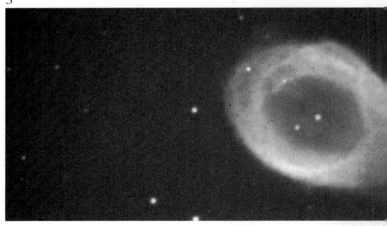
5

1. Infrared radiation from the nebula of Orion.
2. Blue stars in the constellation named Taurus, the Bull. Stars give off different colors from blue to red, depending on their temperature, with blue the hottest.
3., 4. A prominence, or loop of hot gas, on the surface of the sun.
5. Nebula (or ring of gas) produced by the explosion of a supernova, with the nucleus of the star at the center.
6. Nebula remaining from a supernova in the Crab constellation.

2

4

6

31

GALAXIES OF THE UNIVERSE

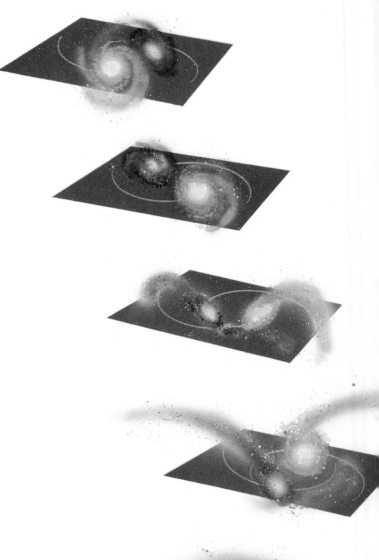

In general, galaxies are not isolated in space. Instead, they tend to form groups of two or three, or larger groups with ten to a hundred or more galaxies. Our galaxy, the Milky Way, belongs to what is called the Local Group.

Just as gravity affects the movement of planets within the solar system, gravity also affects the movement of the galaxies within their groups. Although galaxies, in general, are moving out and away from each other, they are also pulled together by other galaxies within their own group. But just as the planets do not crash into the sun, galaxies do not crash into each other. However, galaxies can come close together. When that happens, stars and gases can hurl outward, and the galaxies can change shape.

Scientists cannot explain all the movements of the galaxies. Some galaxies seem to be pulled by the gravitational force of invisible, "**dark matter**." In fact, this dark matter may make up much more of the universe than we can see.

1. Andromeda, the largest galaxy of the Local Group. (The Milky Way is the second largest.) On clear, dark nights Andromeda can be seen without a telescope.

1

2. Groups of galaxies are seen as elongated shapes. The bright dots are stars of the Milky Way.

3. A possible sequence of events when two galaxies are pulled close together. Long tails are formed as stars and gases are hurled out of their normal orbits. Changes also take place in the nucleus of the galaxy. In some cases, two galaxies can combine to form a single galaxy.

4. In the constellation called Corvus, two galaxies whose shapes have been changed by coming close together.

2

3   4

THE UNIVERSE TODAY

If you look up at the night sky, you might think that stars are more or less evenly spaced throughout the universe. But scientists have found strange patterns. Not only are stars part of galaxies, and galaxies are part of groups, but they also make up huge patterns within the universe.

Galaxies seem to form long threads, with thousands or more in a row. Others form incredibly large patterns that look like walls. The largest structure that scientists have found is called the "Big Wall." It is a gigantic cluster that may be made up of billions of galaxies, and that extends 500 million by 200 million **light-years**. Compared to this immense stretch, it is relatively thin, measuring less than 15 million light-years thick.

Possibly the most interesting feature of the walls is that they seem to encircle gigantic empty bubbles of space. These spaces may in fact not be empty but filled by the "dark matter" that affects the movement of galaxies.

To find out more about the nature of the universe, scientists are attempting to map it. They have already measured distances to millions of galaxies, but they must measure many more to complete the map. One goal of their research is to discover how galaxies formed patterns in space.

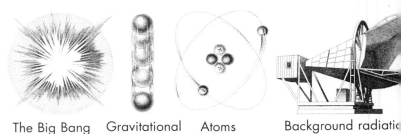

The Big Bang Gravitational force Atoms Background radiatio

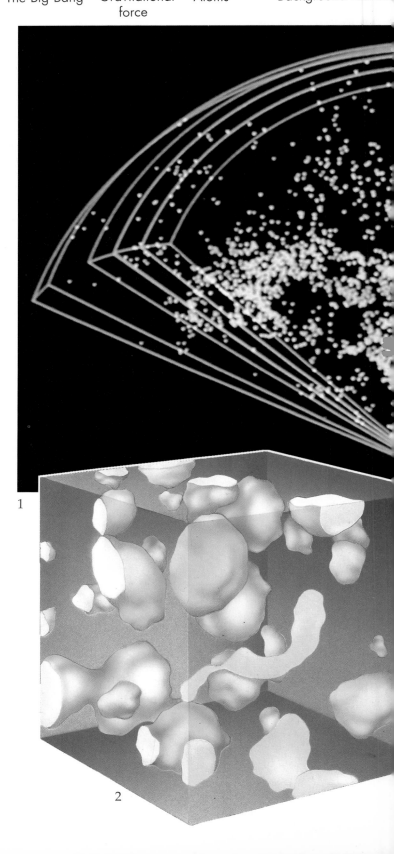

1

2

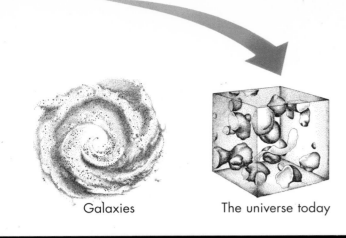

Galaxies   The universe today

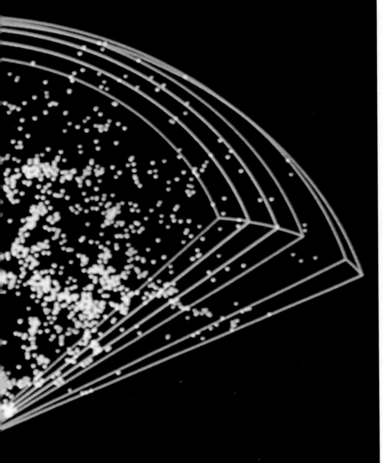

1. Map of a thin band of the sky. Each dot represents a galaxy, with about 4,000 in all. The Milky Way is at the top of the fan, and those farthest away from it are at the bottom. A dense band of galaxies that cuts horizontally through the map represents the Big Wall. Other areas seem to be empty.
2. The structure of the universe can be compared to that of a sponge. Galaxies form walls and threads within the universe, while other parts of it seem to be empty.

ALTERED APPEARANCE

(See illustration on following pages.)

We see stars and other objects in space because they either give off or reflect light. In general, this light travels in a straight path to Earth and all other parts of the universe. But sometimes another object interferes with the light and can change its path. For example, a galaxy that is located between a **quasar** and the Earth can act like a gravitational lens, changing the direction of the light coming from the quasar. When this occurs, we see several images of the same quasar, one for each path of light that reaches us. As a result the quasar appears to be located someplace other than its actual location. In other cases, four images of the actual quasar, called "Einstein's Cross," can be seen. They are given this name because Albert Einstein discovered that the direction of light can be changed by a mass.

Photo of "Einstein's Cross," taken by the Hubble Space Telescope. Four separate images of the single quasar appear on Earth.

See page 35.

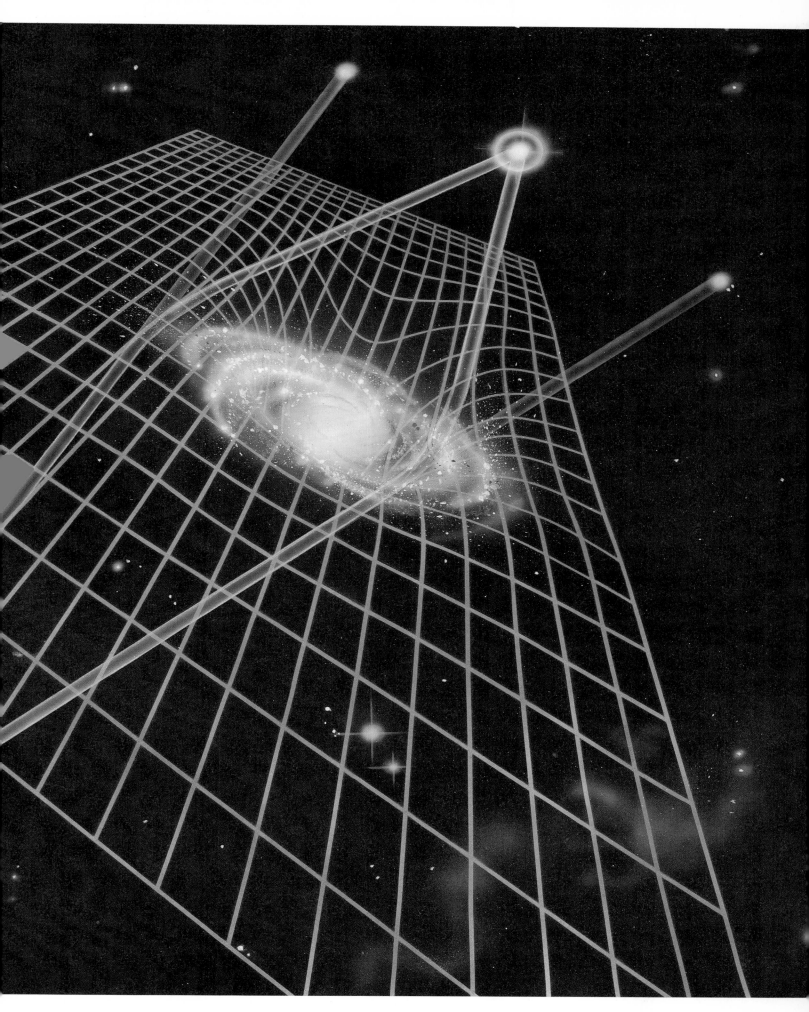

PUSH AND PULL

Scientists believe that the universe is expanding as a result of the explosive force of the Big Bang. This force caused all the matter within the universe to expand, or move outward.

However, the gravitational forces within the universe have the effect of slowing its expansion. We are all very familiar with this force right here on the surface of the Earth. If we throw a ball upward, it naturally falls back to the surface. If we throw it faster, it rises farther. Eventually, it falls back to Earth. If we able to throw it fast enough, it would escape the major part of the Earth's gravitational influence and fly out into space. If we try this same experiment on the moon, the "escape" velocity of the ball would be much smaller, since the moon's mass is so much less than the Earth's.

Scientists today believe that the laws of gravity that we accept to explain our experiences apply throughout the entire universe. Therefore it is possible that the universe will stop expanding and begin to collapse but only if there is sufficient mass present within the universe.

1. Launching of the 1985 *Challenger* space shuttle. A tremendous amount of energy is required to lift a spacecraft above the Earth's atmosphere. Gravity holds the spacecraft in orbit.

2. Model of a Voyager space probe. These probes have been sent to other planets, including Jupiter, Saturn, Uranus, and Neptune. The probes need sufficient momentum to escape the Earth's gravity.

3. An apple falls back down to the ground because it is not thrown with a starting velocity high enough to escape the Earth's gravity. In contrast, the high velocity of a probe allows it to leave the Earth and continue on to other planets.

4. The lunar module of *Apollo 14* on the moon's surface for exploration.
5. On Earth, an apple falls as a result of the pull of gravity.

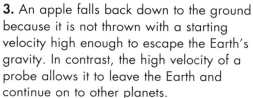

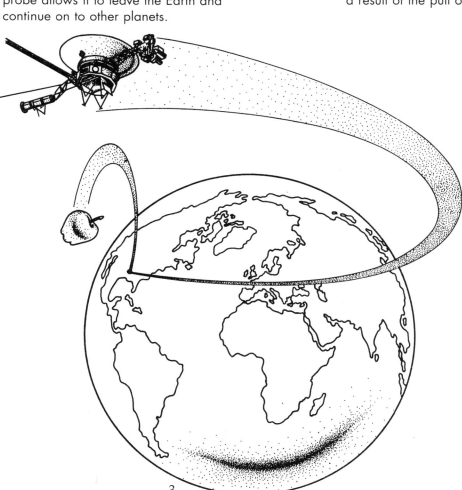

THE FUTURE OF THE UNIVERSE

Using calculations and observations, scientists have refined their theories about the origin of the universe and its evolution. Their next task is to discover whether or not the universe will continue to expand indefinitely.

Counteracting the expanding force of the Big Bang is the force of gravity pulling the universe back together. Right now the influence of the Big Bang explosion is stronger than gravity. The universe is continuing to expand but not as rapidly as it did in the past. At some point in time the force of gravity may be stronger than the force from the Big Bang. Whether or not it will be stronger depends on the amount of mass in the universe, because gravity is related to the amount of mass.

Scientists are now trying to determine how much mass the universe contains. This question is complicated by the puzzle of black holes and dark matter. If large amounts of mass are hidden in these areas, there may be enough gravity to cause the universe to begin to shrink. In this case, the universe would get smaller and smaller, causing the "Big Crunch." At this point it is possible that another Big Bang would occur, and another universe would evolve.

1. The universe today. Its structure, with large gaps, is similar to that of a sponge.
2. The universe is continuing to expand, and the distances between galaxies is increasing.
3. The future of the universe depends on gravity, and therefore, on the amount of mass in the universe. If the mass is great enough, the universe eventually will shrink. If not, the universe will continue to expand.
4. Expansion has stopped, and contraction has begun.
5. Galaxies move closer together.
6. All matter condenses into the Big Crunch and possibly explodes again in another Big Bang.
7. A new and different universe could evolve following another Big Bang.

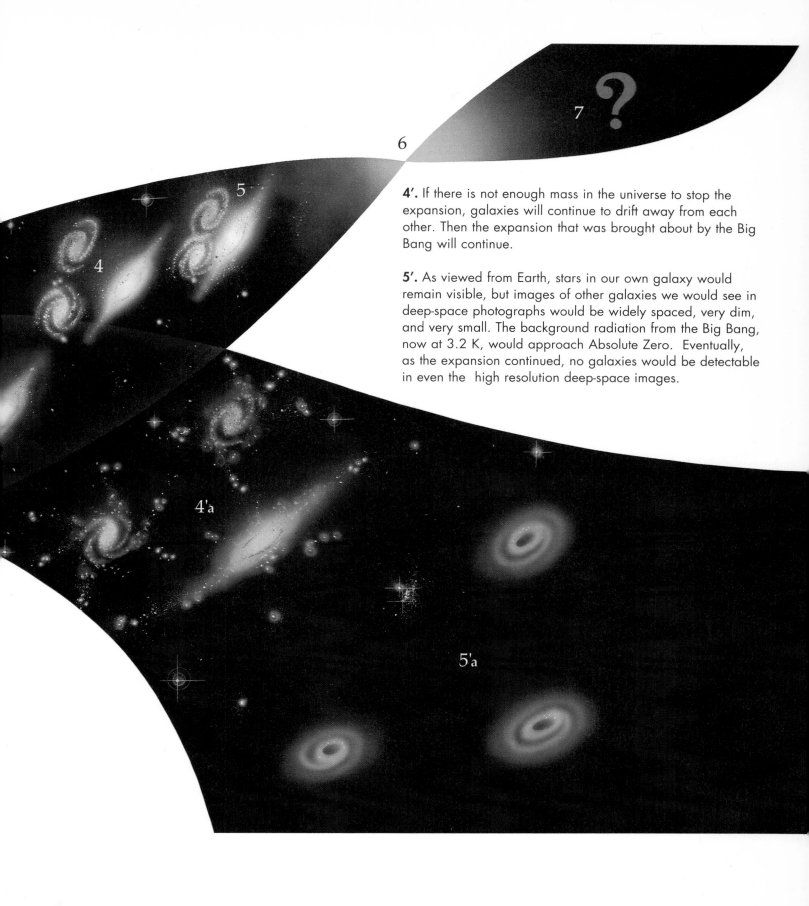

4'. If there is not enough mass in the universe to stop the expansion, galaxies will continue to drift away from each other. Then the expansion that was brought about by the Big Bang will continue.

5'. As viewed from Earth, stars in our own galaxy would remain visible, but images of other galaxies we would see in deep-space photographs would be widely spaced, very dim, and very small. The background radiation from the Big Bang, now at 3.2 K, would approach Absolute Zero. Eventually, as the expansion continued, no galaxies would be detectable in even the high resolution deep-space images.

GLOSSARY

atom: the building block of matter. An atom has a nucleus, containing protons and neutrons, which is surrounded by a cloud of electrons equal in number to the number of protons.

black holes: invisible, former stars that give off no light or other electromagnetic radiation.

constellation: a group of stars that appear close to one another. To people in ancient times they formed pictures in the sky.

dark matter: invisible matter that sends out no electromagnetic radiation, and that may make up nine-tenths of the mass of the universe.

electromagnetic radiation: waves of energy including gamma rays, X rays, ultraviolet rays, visible light, infrared rays, microwaves, and radio waves.

force: a push or a pull. A force can cause an object to change its speed, the direction of its movement, to stop, to begin to move, or to change its shape.

galaxy: a large group of stars, gases, and dust. Galaxies are generally made up of tens or hundreds of billions of stars and are millions of light-years apart from one another.

light-year: a unit that measures astronomical distances. It is the distance light travels in one year. A light-year measures about 6 trillion miles.

mass: the amount of matter in an object. Mass also determines a body's weight.

Milky Way: the galaxy in which the sun and all the stars we normally see are located. Its name comes from the milky band seen on a clear, starry night. The band is formed by the light of countless stars located in the central region of the galaxy.

nebula: a large cloud of gas and dust. Stars can form inside large nebulae.

nuclear reactions: events in which an atomic nucleus interacts with another atomic nucleus or with a particle.

nucleus: the center of an atom, made of protons and neutrons that are bound together by the strong nuclear force.

pulsars: small, rapidly spinning stars that give off bursts of radio signals.

quasars: the extremely bright cores of very distant galaxies.

radio telescopes: large antennae used to collect radio waves from heavenly objects.

red giant: a large, cool star that forms after a major star uses up its hydrogen fuel.

spectrum of light: the various colors that make up white light, arranged according to their wavelengths. By studying the spectra of stars, we can obtain information about the temperature, chemical composition, and movement of the source, as well as about the presence of magnetic fields.

supernova: a massive, exploding star.

telescope: an instrument used to observe heavenly bodies, generally by studying their light. In refracting telescopes, an image is focused through a system of lenses. In reflecting telescopes, an image is focused using a mirror. Sophisticated telescopes record and computers enhance the images.

visible light: the small range of electromagnetic radiation that we are able to see with our eyes.

white dwarf: a small, very hot star that can form after a red giant has used up its fuel.

FURTHER READING

Asimov, Isaac. *How Did We Find Out About the Universe?* Walker, 1983

George, Michael. *Galaxies.* Creative Education, 1993

Herbst, Judith. *Star Crossing: How to Get Around in the Universe.* Macmillan, 1993

Hitzeroth, Deborah. *Telescopes: Searching the Heavens.* Lucent, 1991

Lambert, David. *Stars and Planets,* Raintree Steck-Vaughn, 1994

Rand McNally Staff, *Children's Atlas of the Universe,* Rand McNally, 1990

INDEX

EVOLUTION OF THE MONERAN, PROTIST, PLANT, AND FUNGI KINGDOMS

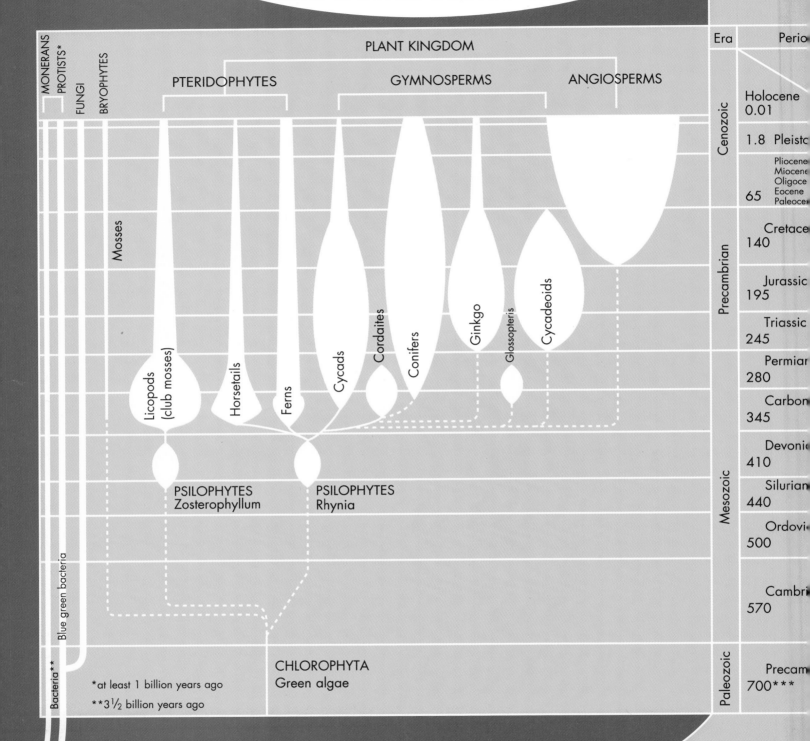

MONERANS
PROTISTS*
FUNGI
BRYOPHYTES

PLANT KINGDOM

PTERIDOPHYTES   GYMNOSPERMS   ANGIOSPERMS

Mosses

Licopods (club mosses)
Horsetails
Ferns
Cycads
Cordaites
Conifers
Ginkgo
Glossopteris
Cycadeoids

PSILOPHYTES
Zosterophyllum

PSILOPHYTES
Rhynia

Blue green bacteria

Bacteria**

CHLOROPHYTA
Green algae

*at least 1 billion years ago

**3½ billion years ago

Era	Period
Cenozoic	Holocene 0.01
	1.8 Pleisto
	Pliocene
	Miocene
	Oligoce
	Eocene
	65 Paleoce
Precambrian	Cretace 140
	Jurassic 195
	Triassic 245
	Permian 280
	Carbon 345
	Devoni 410
Mesozoic	Silurian 440
	Ordovi 500
	Cambri 570
Paleozoic	Precam 700***

EVOLUTION OF THE PROTIST AND ANIMAL KINGDOMS

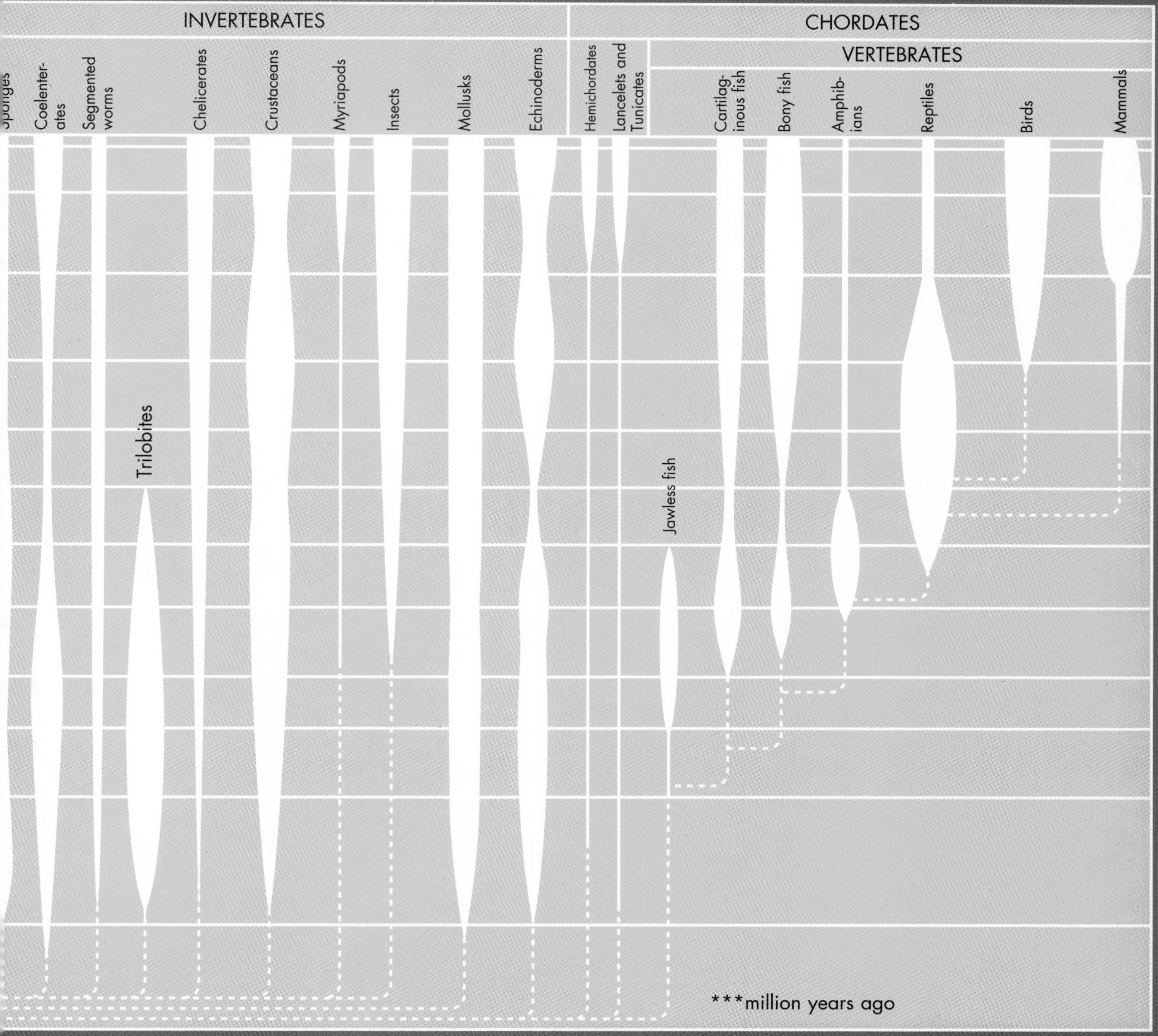

INVERTEBRATES

CHORDATES

VERTEBRATES

Sponges

Coelenterates

Segmented worms

Chelicerates

Crustaceans

Myriapods

Insects

Mollusks

Echinoderms

Hemichordates

Lancelets and Tunicates

Cartilaginous fish

Bony fish

Amphibians

Reptiles

Birds

Mammals

Trilobites

Jawless fish

***million years ago